T0197309

Distorted Visions

TRYING TO GRASP THE GOLDEN RING

Dr. Gayles Evans

DISTORTED VISIONS
TRYING TO GRASP THE GOLDEN RING

iUniverse books may be ordered through booksellers or by contacting:

iUniverse
1663 Liberty Drive
Bloomington, IN 47403
www.iuniverse.com
1-800-Authors (1-800-288-4677)

ISBN: 978-1-5320-7102-7 (sc)
ISBN: 978-1-5320-7101-0 (e)

Print information available on the last page.

iUniverse rev. date: 07/31/2019

**To my dear grandmother
who kept me safe
and loved as a child**

Special Thanks

To my loving family and loyal friends, and to those who seek to find resolution and peace within themselves. Special thanks to my loving granddaughter Dr. Jasmine Evans for her invaluable critique.

Contents

Introduction

I often think about the problems that exist in the world today that debilitate so many people—and even myself at times. These problems often occur because individuals make decisions when they think they are wide awake to reality but are in fact asleep.

There are solutions and alternative ways of handling problems that can control a person, but many people ignore the warning signs and believe there is no problem. It is so easy not to be willing to acknowledge reality, change nefarious behaviors, and accept the right path. One can only speculate as to why many people continue destructive paths and ignore warning signs that indicate their actions are ruining their lives. Some people develop distorted visions because of past experiences or current environments. A distorted vision may develop from past experiences of an individual who has been bullied or sexually, mentally, or physically abused.

Past environmental or current living conditions may cause an individual to become mentally unstable. There are many homeless individuals and families who do not know from night to night where to find a peaceful place to sleep. Many other individuals live in homes with mentally challenged family members. There may be a household member who is violent or is an illicit drug abuser. Negative environmental situations can cause stress and create an unsettling lifestyle. Individuals who are living in an unsettling environment seeking truth on the carousel ride of life may develop mental traps that lock them in dark places where there seem to be no ways to escape.

What is truth? What is real? These questions may never be answered. Finding truth or reality as the mind swirls in an uncontrollable manner, seeking the golden ring, the body might go in the opposite direction, which leads to confusion.

Some individuals seek absolution for their wrongdoings. Others feel they have done nothing wrong and seek no forgiveness. These false beliefs stem from a delusionary state of accepting anything that is contrary to human nature.

The body may react in an unnatural manner when a person believes an experience is real, but the encounter may only be an illusion. Many individuals believe they are wide awake, but they are asleep to reality.

An example of someone believing he or she is wide awake while asleep is when a parent asks a child a question when the child first wakes up. The child answers the question very clearly. Before the child leaves for school, the parent repeats the question. The child responds with the same answer. When the parent asks whether the child remembers being asked the question earlier, the child responds with a negative answer. The child is totally unaware that the same question was asked earlier. The child was still asleep when the question was asked the first time. This happens for many individuals who make decisions when they are not fully awake to reality. When an individual is not awake and makes a bad decision, it may be due to a distorted vision.

Daydreaming

"If you don't design your own life plan, chances are you'll fall into someone else's plan. And guess what they have planned for you? Not much."

—Jim Rohn

Having a distorted vision may lead to daydreaming. Seeking acceptance and happiness by viewing the world through a narrow, deceptive corridor of money, love, sexual gratification, drugs, alcohol, food, or destructive pleasure can be a form of daydreaming. These fantasies can be pleasurable, but they can also be harmful. Individuals who possess distorted vision may trick their minds into believing that obtaining those fantasies can bring them happiness.

The conscious mind is always alert, but when a person is not in a realistic state of mind, awareness of reality can be seen through a hazy, clouded perspective that can cause the individual to view the world with distorted vision. Making unsound decisions to obtain one's fantasies can occur when one has misguided emotional responses.

A study with the goal of teaching individuals how to use daydreams and fantasies to increase empathic abilities was conducted by Frank (1974):

> "Daydreaming can be a creative way of determining whether the person has a clear perspective and understanding of reality and fantasy. Daydreaming can lead to an unrealistic state of mind if an individual believes a fantasy is real."

When someone views the world through a mist of uncertainty or confusion, the world is viewed through one lens instead of two. Individuals may be told that certain situations are not good for their lifestyles, but they will not accept the advice because they do not want to believe what they are pursuing is wrong. This creates an illusion, and the individuals believe they possess a perfect vision of the world. These people try to grasp the golden ring through clouded or hazy vision.

What is the golden ring? The golden ring can mean different things to different people. The golden ring can appear in many forms. Some people are only interested in physical features or smooth conversations. The golden ring could be flashy objects, gold, money, success, fame, or other people. However, those who hold the gold ring of life understand their pasts, have adjusted to negative experiences, and accept that positivity can move them forward in life. The road might not be perfect, but they can move toward to the light without looking back at the dark.

The road of an individual who is seeking the golden ring is paved with good and bad experiences. These experiences can alter the person's goals, achievements, and failures. These issues may create decisions that help the person be in the right place at the right time or the wrong place at the wrong time.

An individual's evaluation of a situation can be based on exposure to a wide array of experiences and decisions. A person who moves through life in a haphazard manner simply flows with the winds of change. This person depends upon events happening in an uncaring way.

The Invisible Child

"If I love you, I have to make you conscious of the things you don't see."

—James Baldwin

When I was five years old, my mother separated from my father, and we had to live with my mother's parents. My mother was sixteen when I was born. She finished high school with a newborn baby and obtained a job as a clerk. I remember my mother working every day except for Saturdays and Sundays.

My mother was a beautiful woman with wavy black hair that framed her brown skin like an angel. She always wore a small amount of makeup because her skin was so smooth. She spoke in a medium voice and smiled often. My mother was an excellent musician. She played every Sunday for the youth service at our church.

I remember returning from school in the evenings and listening to my mother playing the piano or watching her sitting at our old sewing machine with the pedals going up and down as she sewed a dress for me.

Wednesday was showtime. Every Wednesday evening, after I finished my homework, she and I went to the theater. These were happy times in my life, but my mother was very unhappy. She often spent her moments in a restless manner. I did not realize that behind her beautiful smile my mother was hurting inside.

There were dreadful days when my mother would go away and leave me in the care of my grandparents. During this time, my mother developed a drinking problem, which led her into a dark place. Her perceptions of life became cloudy, and she developed a distorted vision. She was never abusive or disrespectful to me or my grandparents, but her absence from home was so apparent. My grandmother would become restless and would not sleep until my mother returned home from her mysterious adventure.

When my mother was home, several of her friends came to our home to visit. I was so happy when my mother came home from work or stayed home on the weekends. My fear and loneness disappeared, and I felt safe.

I was very fond of one of her boyfriends. I felt he was so nice. He reminded me of my dad. He looked so much like my father. I believe that was why my mother was fond of him. On the weekends, he would take my mother and me on long Sunday drives after church. In the summertime, we would go on picnics.

I still had hope that my mother and my dad would reunite, but my dad was married to someone else by then. My thoughts wandered in a whirlwind manner. I thought, "If she marries her new friend, maybe she will be home all the time." However, my wish did not materialize because she married another guy who had a drinking problem.

I did not live with my mother because my grandmother believed it was in my best interests if I continued living with her.

Filling in the Gaps

"The greatest thing in the world is to know how to belong to oneself."

—Michel de Montaigne

My father's family originated in Mississippi. My father's mother was a beautiful woman. She was biracial with Irish, Native American, and African American descent. I thought my father was such a handsome man. He stood about six feet. He had an olive complexion, dark brown hair, and the most infectious smile.

My friends often talked about what their parents were doing as families, and I felt lost in the conversation because I could not compensate for the loss of a true family connection. Because my mother and father were not together, I could only join the discussion by talking about my dad joining the army. I did not want my friends to know my parents were separated.

Before my mother married her friend, we would go to the theater once a week. One evening, my mother told she saw my dad in a newsreel. His leg had been hit by shrapnel. When I went back to school, I told my friends my dad was injured during an attack in the war. He was a hero.

My father's injured leg plagued him for the rest of his life. He was finally discharged from the army because of his injury. The injury caused him to walk with limp and use a cane. My mother told me he had to go in and out of the veterans' hospital for several surgeries, but that did not stop me from believing he was still a handsome man.

I only saw my dad occasionally during my childhood. He would visit us, but my grandfather would not allow him to see me. My grandfather would use profanity and yell, "You can't come in. Go away—and don't come back!"

My father walked down the stairs and left.

Those were terrible days, and I would go to my room and cry all night.

My grandfather believed my father was not good enough for my mother.

I often despaired because I could not see my dad, hear him call me his "nightingale," or feel his touch as his picked me up to give me a hug and a kiss.

"Why? Why? Why?" I was devastated. I wanted to be with my dad, but I was denied that privilege.

My mother often took me to see my father's mother and aunt, but he was never there when we visited their home.

When I was in my twenties, my father and I had a great reunion. We remained very close until his passing.

Was the separation of my father and my mother due to the distorted vision my grandfather had of my father? Many children are separated from their parents because of a lack of communication or the misconceptions of an individual. It makes the children feel invisible. Many children are raised by their grandparents.

Family Affairs

My grandmother and her family were living in Georgia. My grandfather was born in Alabama and traveled to Georgia to seek employment in the decorating business. During the 1900s, the employment opportunities for a black man were limited in the South.

My grandfather met my grandmother when they were only twenty years old. Soon my grandfather created his own decorating business. I regret not asking my grandmother more about how she met my grandfather and about his mother and father. It is so important for children to know their family histories.

I called my grandmother "Mama" and my grandfather "Papa." I called my mother by her name. My grandmother was a tall, beautiful woman who always wore her long gray-black hair braided and pushed back in a bun. She had an olive complexion and grayish eyes. She was part Cherokee, Creek, and African American.

My grandmother's family who were free Native Americans owned land in Georgia. My great-great-grandmother who was Cherokee and Creek, met an African American worker on the family's land and fell in love with him. Soon they married and had four children. My grandmother was the oldest child.

As a young child I remember my grandmother being very sick often because she was having a series of strokes. The family doctor was visiting our home quite often. I was so afraid my grandmother was going to die and leave me alone. When she was not sick, she was walking around the house with the aid of a crutch, mostly cooking, washing my clothes, or preparing me for school. She made sure I did my homework every day.

My grandfather had a dark skin tone, but he had blue-gray eyes. He wore a small mustache, and when he laughed, which was not often, his mustache seemed to move up and down. I used to love to look in his eyes because they would put me in a trance. I remember sitting on his knee as he blew smoke rings from this cigar to make me laugh. My grandparents' children were all born in Georgia.

My mother was only a year old when her parents decided to move to Chicago. My mother's parents had four children: three girls and one boy. Each of my grandparents' children had different personalities. My uncle was the youngest child. He was very quiet, smart, and musically inclined. He worked for the United States government until he died of a heart ailment at the age of twenty-one.

The oldest girl was also a musician like my mother. She wrote beautiful music, played the guitar, and sang on several radio shows. She was tall, had an olive complexion, and always dressed in the latest styles. I remember she always prepared for church on Saturday. Her ritual was to lay out her clothes for the next day, polish her nails, and toes in bright red nail polish. I loved to visit her home as a teenager. The aroma of expensive perfume filled her bedroom and bathroom. She would put a dab of perfume from one of her bottles, which was placed on a fancy glass tray on her dresser, on the inside of my wrist. I felt so grown up. She resembled my grandmother more than the other siblings. I was told that her husband died in a tragic accident. He worked at a gas station, and on the tragic day, someone dropped a cigarette, which set off an explosion. He succumbed to his injuries.

My other aunt, the second oldest daughter, had lighter skin and brown soft hair. Her personality was very disturbing. She was very demanding and stern. Her husband, a very quiet man, worked mostly at night as a cab driver or as a guard at the county jail. He had been a minister in his younger days, but he no longer practiced that profession. I was told my mother was a musician in my uncle's church.

Lost in the Ring

"The first step toward success is taken when you refuse to be a captive of the environment in which you first find yourself."

—Mark Caine

Not having a true family connection created a void in my childhood. I missed my dad so much. Not knowing when I would see my dad brought on a depressing wave of loneliness. Questions flooded my mind, "Where is my father? Why can't my mother and my father be happy together?"

My grandmother and grandfather were very loving and protective of me. My grandparents' home was in a diverse urban area. As a young child, the rooms in our one-level house seemed dark and small. I remember being left in a back room where the darkness filled the room with gloom and sadness.

The only joy I felt during that time was when I was in the care of a loving Italian American family who lived next door. Rosa and Rosalie, the daughters in the family, babysat for me almost every day. Their two-flat building had a grocery store on the first floor, and the family lived on the second floor. I loved the warmth of their home. The smell of the garlic and basil coming from the kitchen created a craving for delicious pasta and tasty pastries. Their home was bright, and classical music filled the air. It was hard for me to go home. Spending time with Rosa and Rosalie was how I learned to develop a taste for wonderful pasta and the sound of beautiful classical music.

At the age of seven, I was very sad when my grandparents decided to move three blocks away to a larger space. Our new home was a three-story building on the south side of town. We lived on the second floor, one of my mother's older sisters and her husband lived on the third floor, and another family lived on the lower level.

The homes in the neighborhood were either single-family homes or two-flat buildings with basements. Several homes were split into several apartments; some families lived in the front apartments, and some families lived in the rear apartments. The neighborhood was relatively safe, but my grandparents were very protective of me. I could only play in front of our home, and when the streetlights came on, I had to be home inside my house.

The new environment was the same as my old neighborhood. Our neighbors were from Greece, Italy, and America. Once a month, a grand parade came down our street, and drums, trumpets, and colorful floats marched through our neighborhood. It was glorious.

Papa's Little Partner

My grandfather was a weekend drunk who worked six days a week as an interior decorator. He never drank alcohol during the week. However, on Saturdays, he would go fishing and enjoy some alcohol with his brother-in-law and some of their friends.

On Sundays, my grandfather and his brother-in-law would faithfully attend church. After church, they would go to the local tavern and get sloppy drunk. That was their weekly routine.

At the age of six, I started visiting the United Methodist Church with my grandfather and his brother-in-law on Sundays. My grandmother never knew my grandfather was taking me to the neighborhood tavern after church. When my grandmother finally found out my grandfather's Sunday routine, my grandfather was in real trouble—and I never saw the inside of the tavern again. I loved my grandfather dearly. He died of prostate cancer when I was ten years old.

Joy in the Day

"Hardships often prepare ordinary people for extraordinary destiny."

—C. S. Lewis

I always had my Saturday mornings to look forward to. I woke up on Saturday mornings with a mixture of joy and dread. I knew my grandmother was going to give me a dose of either castor oil or Black Draught. She always said, "You need the medication to clean you out, so you won't catch get a cold." My joy was that there was no school.

My youngest aunt's personality was very difficult to understand due to her mood swings. I saw her caring side during the daylight hours and her dark, ugly, cruel side at night. My aunt turned everything into a negative situation, and at night, her distorted vision turned into a very dark view of life. She had a twisted view of her family and was very paranoid. However, she was pleasant during the day.

My aunt took me to and from school every day. On the way home, she would stop and chat with the neighbors. On Saturday mornings, when I did not have to take my routine medication. We would go downtown to do her shopping. I looked forward to those special Saturday mornings.

To get downtown, we had to walk about a block to catch the bus on State Street. The bus would take us directly to her favorite stores. Sitting by the window, I would stare at the houses as the bus drove by. I wondered if the families were happy. I watched the children playing, running, and laughing in their yards, I thought, "Were they happy and were they safe?"

As we approached downtown, I stared out the window at the beautiful clothes on the mannequins and dreamed I was wearing the clothes.

My aunt took my hand and pulled me up from my seat. "Time to go", she said. I was still daydreaming about being a beautiful lady in beautiful clothes.

My aunt walked so briskly past the store windows that I almost had to run to keep up with her. As a ten-year-old, I was not very tall. My short legs burned from the pressure of the pace. We finally reached her favorite store, Stop & Shop, and proceeded down the stairs. As we entered the store, the aroma of fresh bread filled the air. The smell made me so hungry, but it did not matter. I knew we would not eat anything until we got home.

My aunt only wanted three things from the store: boiled ham, macaroni salad, and potato salad. I wondered why we had to stand in line for so long before the person behind the counter asked my aunt for her order. We had arrived at the counter before many of the people, but my aunt was passed over until the people who had come in after her were waited on. After my aunt paid for her order, we were off to Woolworths.

Woolworths was a little south of Stop and Shop. The department store sold almost everything, including bakery products. Passing the pretty clothes, we rushed to the back of store to purchase half a pound cake in the bakery. As we approached the counter, there were only a few people. Once again, we had to wait until all the white people had been waited on.

On the bus, I felt tired and unhappy because I was returning to an unhappy home.

Despair in the Night

"I've learned that people will forget what you said.
People will forget what you did, but people will never
forget how you made them feel."

—Maya Angelou

After my aunt's husband left for work, my aunt would become very disturbed. She would pace up and down the stairs, knock loudly on our door, and demand that my grandmother let her in. I believe she demonstrated this cruel behavior at night because my mother's visits at night were far and in between.

My grandmother's movements were very slow and unstable. As we prepared for bed, my aunt came down to our apartment and demanded to be let in. She would storm into the house and explode with anger. Standing in front of my grandmother, she would yell, use profanity, and call us negative names. The verbal abuse would continue until her husband returned from work in the morning.

It was difficult to prepare for school in the morning because I didn't get enough sleep. I was nervous after being called all kinds of names. It was heartbreaking to hear my aunt abusing her mother. My grandmother had developed Parkinson's disease, and she had tremors. My aunt would say, "You old shaky-head b———." She called me a "skinny b———."

Living through abusive experiences as a child affected how I viewed the world as a teenager and an adult. Abuse can cause people to develop distorted vision.

My aunt had a very distorted vision of life, and it never changed.

She died of liver cancer at the age of sixty-four. Her abusive behavior affected my life and caused me to have very low self-esteem.

My aunt also verbally abused her only daughter. Her daughter married an abusive man, and the marriage ended in divorce. She became an alcoholic and developed Parkinson's disease. She died at the age of fifty-seven. Words can be so damaging to the soul.

Trying to Understand

"If you don't design your own life plan, chances are you'll fall into someone else's plan. And guess what they have planned for you? Not much."

—Jim Rohn

Some individuals who have experienced negativity or a disruptive environment still have a clear perspective on life. These individuals hold the golden ring. However, my cousin was not able to move beyond the past. The abuse gave her a distorted vision of reality.

Some individuals with distorted vision appear to be wide awake, but they are asleep to reality. As young adults, we believed what we saw around us was real—even though it was only an illusion.

Actions and emotions are often driven by uncontrollable forces, and many people only believe what they want to believe. I believe my aunt was searching for truth and happiness by performing negative actions. She was motivated by immorality and believed her actions were okay. However, her actions led her family to a destructive path. Individuals who seem heartless and unhappy like my aunt are often drawn by distorted visions that can lead them to dark lifestyles.

I am so sorry my cousin was not able to find real peace and happiness in her life. The pain and anguish she experienced as a child—from her mother's distorted vision—led her to a path of reaching for the golden ring by using alcohol. Searching for truth and trying to escape my worries, I tried to reach for the golden ring by getting married at the age of nineteen and moving away. My grandmother came to live with us in our new home until she passed away at eighty-four years old.

Before my grandmother passed away, she was my son's babysitter while I worked. My husband owned his own business and was away a vast amount of time. Working with various clients, my husband began to drink heavily. Soon, his drinking problem affected our marriage. The memory of my grandfather's drinking disorder and my mother's current drinking problem put an emotion strain on my family. My husband was never abusive when he drank. My constant concern was that our business would fail because of his drinking habit. It haunted me every day.

During the summers, after my son was born, our family would travel to different locations in the United States and Canada. We often visited my husband's family on the East Coast and then drove to Canada. Those were good times. I felt happy, safe, and loved. The lingering memory of my childhood seemed to slip into a small corner of my mind.

My husband passed away from a heart attack when my son was six years old. I was only twenty-six years old. The pain and depression returned in a wave of darkness and loneliness. With the support of family, friends, coworkers, and prayers, the wave of darkness became a path of light. My work became therapeutic. I started working in a managerial position.

My mother was still drinking, and she was having serious medical issues. She began to have serious headaches, and she was tired all the time. I tried to get her to go to the doctor, but she refused.

When my son was eighteen, he began to give her advice. She finally went to see a doctor. My mother was diagnosed with end-stage blood pressure that damaged her heart and kidneys. She had to start dialysis.

Who Am I?

"Life isn't about finding yourself. Life is about creating yourself."

—George Bernard Shaw

Every day, there are choices in life. One choice is related to dietary issues. Distorted vision can lead to poor dietary choices. It can be easy to make the wrong choice about having a second slice of chocolate cake when a person is on a diet or has a medical condition that forbids chocolate. A favorite dessert can be eliminated from a person's diet, but a thought is lurking: "Just a small piece."

Medical professionals often advise the public that certain foods are not good for maintaining a healthy diet, but consumers continue to eat the wrong foods. The distorted vision can lure individuals into thinking certain foods or spices are tasty and that a little bit will not hurt their health.

Food warnings are given to aid consumers because they can be harmful. Experts agree that nutrition directly affects mental, emotional, and physical functions. A poor diet is often linked to cancer, cardiovascular disease, diabetes, anemia, and digestive disorders (Vail & Cavanaugh 2010). If you are eating a food that is damaging to your health, can you stop?

Food Is Not the Answer

"I care for myself. The more solitary, the more friendless, the more unstrained I am, the more I will respect myself."

—Charlotte Brontë

From a variety of reasons, my blood pressure was out of control. With a reading of 264/117, I was rushed to the emergency room and was immediately admitted to the hospital. The doctor tried several medications, but my blood pressure was still unstable. After several attempts to reduce it with a combination of medications, I became stable and was sent home.

The distorted vision of eating certain foods with salt, which I believed was so tasty, before entering the hospital was still strong in my mind. The doctor told me to eliminate salt from my diet, but I believed food could not be eaten without some form of salt. Salt became my golden ring.

This distorted vision of adding salt to food placed me in a dangerous position. I kept eating salt alternatives without realizing it was not the solution. The distorted vision deceives the taste buds and sends the message that some form of salt must be used. After several consultations with the doctor, I realized there should be no form of salt in my diet. Unhealthy eating habits can be controlled by trying to reach the golden ring of satisfaction.

Someone who is unhappy or disappointed can form addictive relationships with food. Food can become an enabling tool that alleviates stress. The emotional relief is equated to the taste and visual appearance of food. Food can replace the feelings of being lonely, unloved, unforgiven, neglected, or abused. The ritual is repeated, and the new habit of craving food is created, which leads to a false sense of satisfaction.

The satisfaction transforms into a belief that reaching for the golden ring through obsessive eating will solve the problem. As this habit is formed, the ring swings farther out of reach, causing frustration and driving the person into a toxic state of mind. The golden ring is only a smoke screen that is viewed by the individual through blurry, hazy vision. Seeking food is a tool to release satisfaction—like riding a carousel—and the individual stretches out to reach the golden ring. They touch the ring, but they never fully grasp it. I was very blessed to have a friend at work who started bringing me fresh herbs from he and his wife's garden to help me overcome the taste of salt in my meals.

One can view the ring like consuming excessive amounts of red meat, fatty foods, doughnuts, chocolate, coffee, salt, sugar, cigarettes, drugs, and alcohol. It temporarily tricks the mind into satisfaction and relaxation. However, the stressful situation still exists, the carousel is still turning, and the golden ring is still out of reach.

How great is the pleasure of looking at a second bowl of pasta or a box of chocolates when in a stressful frame of mind? Before you are totally aware of how much you have consumed, the box of chocolates is completely empty. Viewing of the world through a distorted vision, the golden ring transforms itself into the chocolate.

The individual cannot see or realize the adverse consolations of obesity, diabetes, coronary artery disease, high blood pressures, type 2 diabetes, stroke, and other health issues that can occur from having a distorted vision. People who are not aware of healthy foods and rely only on what looks good or tastes good cannot maintain healthy lifestyles.

An unhealthy diet will not replace the missing elements in life. The brush of reality must swipe across the lens so the whole view is displayed. Healing can only begin when people stop reaching out for the golden ring.

Food addiction can affect an individual in the same way a person can be addicted to drugs. Food addiction involves the brain's neurotransmitters and acts like a drug. Gunnar Rundgren identified several signs of food addiction:

- You often feel guilty after eating certain foods, yet you continue to eat them.
- You often hide your consumption of unhealthy foods from others.
- You make excuses about why you should eat something.

Physical, emotional, social, and spiritual happiness and well-being are all affected by food addiction. Not all food addictions result in weight gain. With bulimia, individuals consume large amounts of food and vomit or use laxatives to eliminate what has been eaten. With anorexia, excessive eating is followed by limiting food for days or weeks.

Impulsive eating habits are often triggered by mood changes. Anger, sadness, and anxiety can trigger episodes of overeating (Jane 2010).

There are many resources to help with compulsive eating disorders. The Comprehensive Overeating Recovery Effort (CORE) helps individuals develop a clear lens through medically supported programming in non-diet weight management. It fuses mental health, dietary support, education, exercise/movement, and medical management (https: www.eatingrecoverycenter.com). An individual should always consult a physician for safe steps to correct any disorder.

Another way to kick the bad habit of overeating is to replace the unhealthy routine with a new healthy habit. The eating disorder remains in the brain, but one must strive to choose good behavior over bad behavior (Vines 2012). Self-perception is another element that individuals can view with a distorted vision.

Learning to Love Myself

"Even the models we see in magazines wish they could look like their own image."

—Cheri K. Erdman

Mirrors can reflect an out-of-focus perception of self. After enduring my aunt's behavior, I developed low self-esteem. I started to believe all her negative words about my physical appearance. Negative words become ingrained in children's minds, and they begin to believe the negative words. Calling a child fat, skinny, or dumb sticks to the mind like glue.

Some people judge their own physical image through the eyes of others or social media. The images on social media are false. Social media standards are based on a perfect human. These are false standards. Social media focuses on physical size, shape, height, skin color, hair texture, eyes, nose, and physical features.

Comparing oneself with others can cause a state of disillusionment. A pretty face or perfect body is measured by the media, which often promotes a certain product. Some people compare media images with their physical features by using social media. There is no perfect body or perfect face. No one should compare their own physical appearance to another person because everyone is physically different. No one has the right to call someone undesirable or ugly. No one has the right to judge someone by their skin color, hair texture, or facial or physical features.

Some individuals undergo plastic surgery because they believe the reflection in the mirror displays flawed elements and try to correct unrealistic flaws. Many of these individuals are misguided and believe plastic surgery must be performed. These surgeries can lead to deformity or death. This is another way of grasping for the golden ring through hazy distorted vision, which can be dangerous. These individuals are viewing themselves through a distorted vision.

Psychiatrist Jamie D. Feusner suggests that sufferers may have lost the ability to see the entire self, causing general perceptual deficit. Many undergo repeated cosmetic surgeries and struggle to form meaningful personal relationships, and the risk of suicide is high (Schreiber 2012). Physical appearance may be clouded by media images of what is perceived as beautiful or acceptable.

Some movies and television shows portray minorities in a discriminatory manner by using the "brown paper bag test." The entertainment industry still uses the paper bag test for judging talent (those who are darker than a paper bag does not get certain roles). Dark-skinned women and men portray servants or criminals. Many producers cast lighter-skinned women as married and successful leading ladies. Lighter-skinned men are the good guys with white hats, and darker-skinned men are cast as drug dealers, pimps, bad guys, and jokers.

To enhance their appearances to reflect what the media suggests as acceptable in society, many women bleach their skin or perm their hair. They wear weaves or wigs to have so-called good hair. The brown paper bag test does not judge natural beauty. Some actors are not allowed to display their talents, and studios display darker-skinned individuals as second-class citizens. Their talents are judged with a distorted view.

Stereotyping minorities when selecting actors often occurs with white and African American filmmakers. The casting process is often done in a discriminatory way based upon skin color. When films are shown, it gives the public a certain image to emulate.

How do individuals view themselves and the world around them? A person's self-image is often misguided. Confusing signals are transmitted to the consciousness. These images are illusions.

Some people think believing is seeing. The statement is often used out of context. Should an individual always believe what they see? Is the individual viewing the situation with a clear vision or a distorted vision? A person's viewpoint might not always be true. Life experiences can be viewed and judged through a distorted vision.

Some individuals make judgments based upon physical appearance. No one has the right to judge another person's individual's appearance. The person's beauty standards could be misleading. People have no right to judge anyone else. Judging someone can lead to mistrust, misconceptions, discrimination, and animosity. Some individuals judge others based upon appearances. Some individuals love and admire the wrong people because of appearances.

The way a person views their environment determines how they function. A person who had negative experiences or lived in a negative environment might have low self-esteem, low self-confidence, insecurity, or paranoia. Certain situations create a false sense of joy, enlightenment, or trust. In these cases, the real world is replaced by a fantasy world.

Individuality is wonderful and should be cherished. It is not always easy to say, "I know who I am," "I am beautiful," "I am a good person," or "I believe in myself."

There are individuals who are raised in loving environments but are bullied in school or the workplace. Negative responses can often strip an individual's self-esteem. Negative words from parents, guardians, or caregivers can be destructive. Hate-filled words create a double vision of reality that strips away the individual's identity and creates a negative reality for the person. Confidence is taken away, and a new reality is formed, which leads to low self-esteem.

My aunt's verbal abuse when I was a child affected my self-esteem. There are many children who are told they are not beautiful, they are skinny, or they are overweight. These negative words are ingrained in the minds of children and may cause them to have false images of themselves.

Negative words can also affect adults. Many adults are humiliated, bullied, and degraded. They believe they do not fit into society. They believe they are not important, which creates a distorted vision. The person's identity is lost, and a new person is created with a negative view of themselves. This can lead to the person indulging in excessive drinking, drug abuse, and bullying.

Looking through a distorted vision can create someone who sees others from a negative perspective. When one has distorted vision, that person believes people who do not mirror what they look like or have the same philosophical beliefs do not deserve respect or acceptance.

If the person does not mirror who they are—via ethnicity, race, or religious beliefs—the person is considered not equal. Those negative beliefs reflect discrimination.

Rejection! Rejection! Discriminatory Behaviors: We Are One World

"Believe in yourself! Have faith in your abilities! Without a humble but reasonable confidence in your own powers, you cannot be successful or happy."
—Norman Vincent Peale

Discrimination includes intolerance based on age, ethnicity, race, religion, disability, or sexual orientation. Individuals who believe other minority groups are unequal have a distorted vision. Prejudice is hostility toward a group of people. It is usually based on stereotypes. Negative judgments lead to discrimination.

The word *stereotype* comes from the Greek word meaning "solid," which is a simplified description applied to every person in a category. Stereotyping leads to discrimination. The practice of discrimination must be stopped. A child is born with a clear vision without reaching for any golden ring.

A child's ability to interact with another child is normal. A child does not judge another child by ethnicity, religion, or social status—unless he or she has been taught discrimination. As a child, my Italian neighbors were very loving to me. I loved them too. They saw me as a child—regardless of my race—who they could take care of and love. The family have a clear vision. Treating me as one of the family gave me a sense of warmth and safety with people who looked different from me. This clear vision came from my mother and my grandmother when they opened her home to students from Wheaton College every week. They only saw people—not race, ethnicity, or religion.

My father finally divorced and married a lovely woman from Germany. After my father passed away, I stayed in touch with my stepmother until she passed away.

To accept minority individuals as equal, one must have a clear vision. Some people are taught to stereotype other people and form negative views based on age, ethnicity, race, religion, disability, or sexual orientation. When someone begins to stereotype someone, they have a distorted vision of the world.

Acting upon the belief that minorities are unequal, an individual's views of life turn negative. These reactions are often reinforced by social media. Movies, television shows, and social media portray minorities as negative characters. With a clear lens, people treat minorities with respect. When discrimination disappears, equality is obtained.

Some movies and television shows depict minorities as criminals, lazy, irresponsible, prostitutes, or people who are unfit to function in society. Children can form negative judgments about minorities because of peers, parents, or social media. Negative images of minorities can create an unfair view of minorities. People can view them as unworthy.

Equality is important for every individual in the world. An individual with distorted vision judges everyone according to their own set of standards, values, and rules. An individual with a distorted vision believes minorities do not meet their standards. An individual with a distorted vision views minority as unfit to function in society and will not treat them equally. These misguided individuals create hostile environments for minorities and often engage in violence.

Employers with distorted visions often do not consider minorities for jobs. They cannot admit the decision was based on age, race, ethnicity, or religious or sexual orientation because of the law, but the second interview never occurs. Many employment agencies will call individuals who are seeking jobs online and ask, "What year did you graduate from high school?" If the individual states a certain year that indicates they are a senior citizen, the caller will hang up. Some minorities and senior citizens are lower-class individuals.

Minorities experience discrimination in classrooms, politics, churches, workplaces, restaurants, and malls. Discrimination affects promotions and pay.

Many minority children from diverse urban communities never encounter segregation until they explore other parts of their cities. Thirty years ago, shopping downtown was an exciting adventure for a young adult. However, when minorities entered a store, they frequently became uncomfortable and lost that feeling of joy and excitement. The wonderful feeling was replaced with a negative feeling. Individuals who view minorities as invading their environments have a distorted vision.

Many minority shoppers are followed around stores as if they were going to do something wrong. They must wait for all nonminority customers to be served. They are often be the last people served. Some stores create unwelcoming atmospheres. This form of discrimination is not as obvious as it was thirty years ago, but it still exists. The cold treatment and exclusion can create insecurity for minorities. Some believe they are not equal in society. The habit of minorities being followed in stores is still being practiced today.

Some minorities do not understand their rich heritage and their important contributions to society. They should walk with pride and understand the accomplishments of minorities. The achievements of minorities are often hidden, and some stories will never be told. There are thousands of success stories that need to be taught in schools. There are minority inventors, medical professionals, entertainers, athletes, scholars, construction workers, chefs, caregivers, and trailblazers.

To begin the process of removing a distorted vision, an emphasis must be placed on the self. Everyone must look inside themselves, try to understand what they see, and accept the findings. Admitting personal bias is the first step. Accept who you are and how you see the world. Accept those who look different or speak differently. The veil of deception must fall away and reveal that all people—regardless of race, ethnicity, age, disability, religious belief, or sexual orientation—should be treated with respect.

Fanatical religious beliefs can cause people to become discriminatory or intolerant. A fanatical person goes beyond what is reasonable. Individuals with distorted views of religious values and beliefs cannot accept someone else's religious choices. Extremist religious groups are often referred to as cults. These extremist groups' activities often lead to dangerous outcomes for the leaders and followers. There are those who believe there is no higher power than their own consciousness.

Some religious organizations hold up the Bible as a guideline for enforcing discrimination. Some individuals believe in a higher power but reject the idea that Jesus was the Son of God. Others believe he was just a prophet who demonstrated the ways humans should live. People's beliefs should be respected if they are not harmful to others. Individuals with distorted vision believe their way is the only way.

Life is a cycle of events, and each step in the cycle can be viewed with clear or distorted vision. The life cycle is a colorful array of blooming colors: black, white, brown, yellow, and tan. Some colors are more brilliant, and some are fading. Regardless of the brightness, the colors give the environment a sparkling light to guide people through the cycle. If the light cannot be seen, the journey through life is dark, rough, and unstable.

Individuals who have distorted vision cannot reach for the golden ring because they view the world as a place where only "their kind" should live. The light and beauty of the sparkling light is hidden. Discrimination is a path of darkness and loneliness that hides the light and beauty of diversity.

Drug and Alcohol Abuse

"If you fell yesterday, stand up today."

—H. G. Wells

Living with my grandfather and mother who abused alcohol was very frightening. I believe my childhood was more affected by my mother's drinking habit than my grandfather's habit. Not knowing when my mother was coming home and fearing for her safety were my main concerns.

I hated the idea of her putting on her makeup because I knew she was going out for the night—and I not know when she would return. I now know she was lonely and missed my dad.

The awareness that night was approaching was scary. I hoped the walls would close around my grandmother and me and separate us from my aunt's furious rages that made the nights unbearable for us.

My mother's alcohol use created several medical problems in her body. She had to start dialysis and eventually lost her legs. With the help of my son, my daughter-in law, my middle granddaughter, and a wonderful caregiver, we took care of my mother until she passed away at the age of eighty. My mother's personality never changed during her illness. She was a loving and caring person. Everywhere my mother went, she created friends. Her dialysis treatment center at the hospital gave her an eightieth birthday party two months before her death.

Alcohol abuse has a way of making a person unreliable and unsteady. Addiction can be a result of loneliness, stress, anxiety, pain, depression, or trauma. I often wonder why my grandfather and my mother drank. My mother stopped drinking when she became very ill, but my grandfather never stopped and died of prostate cancer. My grandfather and mother were never abusive to anyone when they were under the influence of alcohol. They were loving and extremely friendly. I believe they drank because of their friends, and my mother drank because of her unhappiness, but I am only speculating about those reasons.

In 2017, Dr. Rachel Lipari identified seven reasons for drug abuse:

- self-medicating for anxiety, trauma, and/or stress
- adolescence
- depression
- peer pressure
- feeling good
- availability
- gateway drugs

Self-dissatisfaction may result in dysfunctional behaviors. Substance abusers see themselves as hazy, cloudy, or out of focus. Self-esteem drops, and some individuals turn to drugs and alcohol. Dysfunctional behavior is not limited to adults. It affects all ages, races, ethnicities, and genders. Substance abuse for poor minorities can result in family disruption, single parenthood, segregation, social isolation, and unemployment. Environmental influences related to poverty can cause substance abuse.

Why do individuals try to reach for the golden ring through drug abuse? A distorted vision gives them the idea that life cannot be controlled. Self-conflict and dissatisfaction overcome goals and dreams. Whites and Native Americans have the highest levels of alcohol use during adolescence and adulthood (Mosher and Scott). Native Americans have high levels of alcohol abuse and drugs, which is often due to frustration, alienation, low self-esteem, and hopelessness (Caltano 1998).

Individuals with distorted vision who abuse alcohol do not have a clear image. Their lenses are often clouded with anger, disillusion, low self-esteem, or misguided beliefs. Their behavior affects their entire families. Many individuals who abuse alcohol or drugs are violent. The abusive behaviors toward their victims are often uncontrollable, and there is no remorse because the predator believes their actions are right. The sorrow, embarrassment, fear, and mental and physical pain are real and affect the abusers and their families. Many abusers cannot find the golden ring and seek strength and comfort in drugs or alcohol, which often leads other family members to some form of abuse.

According to the National Institute of Drug Abuse, drugs that are commonly misused are opioids, depressants (including tranquilizers, sedations, and hypnotics), and stimulants. Drug overdoses resulted in nearly fifteen thousand deaths in 2008.

Prescription drug abuse has increased in the past fifteen years. After alcohol, marijuana, and tobacco, prescription drugs are the next most popular drug for twelfth graders.

Most adults between fifty-seven and eighty-five years of age use at least one prescription medication daily, which can lead to incorrect usage. The misuse of medications can lead to an increase in emergency room visits.

Many behavior centers and websites contain information about treating drug addiction (https://www.drugabuse.gov, 877-NIDA-NIH, and 240-645-0228).

Individuals who abuse alcohol or drugs are often bullied or become bullies. Some drug abusers become violent with their companions because of distorted vision. They often seek to control and dominate their environments by bullying their way through life. Their objective is to control their victims through bullying and harassment—physically, mentally, or both. There are many forms of bullying, including cyberbullying, which can exist in religious settings as well as public and private sectors.

Bullying was part of my childhood. My aunt did not indulge in the use of drugs or alcohol, but she bullied my grandmother and me because she knew we were weak and unable to defend ourselves. She felt power and control as she yelled and shouted profanities at us. Believing we were the ones who were weak made her feel powerful, but she was the weak one and had distorted vision.

Bullying

"Never be bullied into silence. Never allow yourself to be made a victim. Accept no one's definition of your life but define yourself."

—Harvey Flerstein

Bullying can be committed by children, young adult, or adults. A bully is a dysfunctional individual. The victim can be known to them or randomly selected. Bullying is often caused by a predator who was bullied in the past. Predators can be male or female.

Bullies can use sarcastic remarks, verbal discrimination, teasing, and physical abuse to intimidate their victims. The US Senate hearings on media and violence concluded the following:

- Violent television, movies, video games, and music significantly increase the likelihood of aggressive behavior.
- They lead to short-term and long-term effects.
- The effects are real, lasting, and substantial.

At present, no federal laws directly address bullying. In some cases, bullying overlaps with harassment, which is covered under federal civil rights laws. Some states have antibullying laws and policies. Illinois treats cyberbullying as a class B misdemeanor. No matter what label is used—bullying, hazing, or teasing—schools are obligated to address conduct that is severe, pervasive, or persistent. Bullying creates hostile environments in schools, homes, workplaces, and churches.

Many children have committed suicide because they were the victims of bullying. Fights in elementary schools have caused children to die.

Misguided individuals can create havoc for themselves and for others. Someone with distorted vision can create abusive behavior that include slander, exclusion, stalking, bullying, sexual harassment, and cyberbullying to those they disagree with or dislike for a variety of reasons.

In several school shootings, the shooters were victims of bullying. Even some survivors of school shootings have committed suicide. Children and young adults who are suffering silently from the abuse of being bullied are becoming more common in society. Many of these children commit suicide because they are unable to live with the torment waged upon them. There must be a path of hope for these children.

Cyberbullying

Cyberbullying—text messages, emails, social networking sites, videos, websites, and fake social media profiles—is a common source of bullying. Social media is an avenue for posting malicious or derogatory pictures or messages. These negative words and/or pictures give a sense of shame and fear to victims. Cyberbullying can lead to suicides. When a child or an adult is slandered on social media, it can lead to a maze of self-destruction. Many dangers lurk in cyberspace and in face-to-face bullying.

The internet has changed how information is received and transmitted. When a new generation of internet users seeks information or sends information via email or in a chat room, it is often done without precautions or awareness of unforeseen dangers. Cyberbullying is a form of stalking.

Stalking

Stalking is a form of bullying. It is a pattern of repeated and unwanted attention, harassment, contact, or other conduct directed at a specific person that would cause a reasonable person to feel fear. The Violence against Women Act extended the federal interstate stalking statute to include cyberstalking.

Stalking can include the following:

- repeated, unwanted, intrusive, and frightening communications from the perpetrator by phone, mail, and/or email
- repeatedly leaving or sending victim unwanted items, presents, or flowers
- following or waiting for the victim at home, school, or work
- direct or indirect threats to harm the victim, the victim's children, relatives, friends, or pets
- damaging or threatening to damage the victim's property
- harassing the victim through the internet
- posting information or spreading rumors about the victim on the internet, in public places, or by word of mouth
- obtaining personal information about the victim via public records, search engines, or private investigators
- going through the victim's garbage, following the victim, or contacting the victim's friends, family, coworkers, or neighbors

Viewing society through an unclear and unfocused lens provides a narrow view and a negative sense of society. The viewer believes there is no other way to function in society. Internet stalking includes cell phones, computers, tablets, social media sites, text messages, chat rooms, and websites. The predators conceal their identities and used the internet as a weapon.

One in six women (16.2 percent) and one in nineteen men (5.2 percent) in the United States will experience stalking at some point. Unwanted telephone calls and text messages are the most common tactics for both female and male victims of stalking.

Do Federal Laws Apply to Bullying?

Bullying transcends age, disability, economic status, ethnicity, gender, language, race, and religion. Individuals without computers in their homes can access the internet from businesses, family members' homes, libraries, neighbors' homes, schools, or other locations. Individuals with access to the internet can receive, transmit, and view information. Users may not be informed about how to be safe in cyberspace.

Are some internet users violating the First Amendment? Who is monitoring your conversations? Users must also be cognizant of who owns the material on the internet.

Sexual Harassment

"Don't be afraid for I am with you. Don't be discouraged for I am your God. I will strengthen you and help you. I will hold you up with my victorious right hand."

—Isaiah 41:10

Recently, Hollywood actors, producers, political leaders, television hosts, and other male celebrities have been accused of approaching women in unwelcome and unsavory manners. These accusations have been made against men for many years, but the women have been ignored or made out to be villains. Many rape victims are afraid to report incidents because officials believe there was no rape or say the woman provoked the action. The #MeToo movement has inspired many women to come forth and expose the predators who have sexually harassed them for years. The distorted vision of these men has come to light, and a movement to support women who have been sexually harassed has been established.

Sexual harassment refers to comments, gestures, or physical contact of a sexual nature that are deliberate, repeated, and unwelcome (Macionis 2017). Sexual harassment violates the Civil Rights Act of 1964, which applies to employers with fifteen or more employees, including state and local governments.

Sexual harassment can occur in a variety of circumstances:

- The victim may be a woman or a man.
- The harasser can be a supervisor.

- The victim may not know the harasser.
- The harasser's conduct is unwelcome.

Quid pro quo means "something for something" in Latin. Hostile work environments can ignore sexual harassment. Quid pro quo harassment takes place when a superior requires sex, sexual favors, or sexual contact from an employee or job candidate as a condition of employment. Sexual harassment increases stress for victims, which can lead to a variety of physical ailments:

- inability to focus on doing a job correctly and safely
- inability of coworkers and managers to effectively respond to or deal with sexual harassment

Intimidation can cause victims to be reluctant to raise legitimate safety issues out of fear of being ridiculed. Workplace violence and harassment can take the form of actual or threatened physical contact. These individuals have distorted vision. The perpetrators are viewing the world through a form of distortion, which is a form of bullying. They believe the act of sexual harassment is causing no harm for their victims.

Sexual harassment and violence are not new. Sexual coercion was a feature of chattel slavery, and African American women endured it without any protection from the law. In the late nineteenth and early twentieth centuries, female employees in manufacturing and clerical positions experienced sexual relations ranging from assault to all manners of unwanted physical or verbal advances (Seigel 2003).

During the nineteenth and early twentieth centuries, the Women's Christian Temperance Movement worked to protect women from sexual harassment. In 1975, activists at Cornell University coined the term *sexual harassment.*

The Center for Disease Control's National Intimate Partner and Sexual Violence Survey in 2010 revealed that 9.4 percent of women have been raped by intimate partners.

Violence against Women, Men, and Children

"You are not what others think you are. You are what God knows you are."

—Shannon Alder

As a survivor of child abuse, I relate to and empathize with those who are hurting from being subjected to any form of neglect, intolerance, or violent behavior.

One Sunday, I was ironing a dress at my aunt's home. I was evidently not ironing as fast as she wished. All at once, she shouted, "What's taking you so long?" She pulled a small dinner knife out of the kitchen cabinet and cut my arm.

The pain from the abuse remains deep down in my spirit and never leaves. It smothered a small corner of my heart. On social media, I have heard many stories about missing children who have been found dead. Recently, the heartbreaking news emerged of a five-year-old child who was beaten to death by his parents and buried in a shallow grave. The frequency of these stories of children being physically abused or killed by parents or boyfriends' stabs at the heart of a nation.

Abusive behavior is a general term for aggressive, coercive, or controlling behaviors that are used to control domestic partners, children, or other victims. If someone admires another individual only for their physical features, they might have a false perception of that individual's personality or moral values. Acceptance of someone can be based on how the person looks. An individual may believe that the person is perfect, and this illusion can last for years or a lifetime.

When the person finally becomes aware of the individual's true personality, clarity may occur, but sometimes it is too late to prevent a tragedy. The illusion often does not change to reality. For some individuals, the illusion remains intact. The distorted vision creates blurry, crooked, hazy, clouded, narrow, or dim vision, and they are always trying to please their "false perfect one." A person with a false sense of happiness will never be happy because their dream person is only perfect in their eyes. When the vision becomes clear and broad, the illusion of seeing a golden ring transforms into reality—and the ring becomes brass, tarnished, and insatiable.

No one can totally evaluate another individual's personality. The observer may be viewing that person with a distorted vision. Judging another individual with a distorted vision may occur in the wrong arena or with the wrong timing. When one is not aware of reality, the way that individual relates to the world cannot be assessed. Observations of another person's life are only speculation. Distorted vision can create a scenario where the wrong ring on the carousel is chosen.

The dreamboat's personality is an illusion, and at some point, in the relationship, a new personality arises. The dreamboat becomes a predator. Some predators blame others for their failures and unhappiness.

John Stuart Mill wrote, "Men do not want solely the obedience of women; they want their sentiments. All men, except the most brutish, desire to have in the woman mostly nearly connected with them, not a forced slave but a willing one; not a slave merely, but a favorite."

Some victims become involved with companions who they think will fulfill all their needs. Many people seek companionship with the first person who pays attention to them. They do not understand why the relationship only lasts for a short period of time. The relationship is formed with a dysfunctional lens.

When a person is seeking love and empathy, the moment when

someone notices them is wonderful. This can be a result of low self-esteem. They believe the ring is within reach. Many of these relationships are built on infatuation. Infatuation is an intense but short-lived passion or admiration.

Michelle Drew said, "Infatuation is an expectation of blissful passion without growth and development. There is often a lack of trust, lack of commitment, and a lack of reciprocity."

Abusive relationships often result in unwanted pregnancies, domestic violence, and bullying. Some babies are abused or killed by fathers or boyfriends. Others are victims of child abuse or sexual abuse, including incest. Many of the women are scapegoats.

In the United States, twenty-four people per minute are victims of rape, physical violence, or stalking by an intimate partner. That equals more than twelve million women and men over the course of a year. Nearly three in ten women (29 percent) on one in ten men (10 percent) in the United States have experienced rape, physical violence, and/or stalking by a partner.

National Domestic Violence

Many women try to defend themselves against predators. These women are graceful, respectful, caring, intelligent, beautiful, strong, and defensive. Female swans are graceful and beautiful and have strong protective instincts for their babies. They are known for their fierce temperaments and strong wings. The black swan from Australia can swim on one leg and remain aware of predators. A mother swan is very protective of her babies. Male swans often underestimate female swans by assuming they are weak.

Some women fall prey to men's abusive behaviors because they have distorted visions of themselves. These women are often beaten. Many have low self-esteem and feel worthless or ashamed. Many are bullied or killed.

Many predators view their abusive actions as acceptable. They believe they are making the world a better place. They believe their abusive actions are not wrong.

The Women's Rural Advocacy Programs studied child and spousal abuse in the United States:

- Children in homes where domestic violence occurs are physically abused or seriously neglected at a rate 1,500 percent higher than the national average in the general population.
- Lenore Walker's 1984 study found that mothers were eight times more likely to hurt their children when they were being battered than when they were safe from violence.

- A major study of more than nine hundred children at battered women's shelters found that nearly 70 percent of the children were themselves victims of physical abuse or neglect.

Lynn S. Levey, Martha Wade Steketee, and Susan L. Keilitz released "Lessons Learned in Implementing an Integrated Domestic Violence Court: The District of Columbia Experience" in 2000. Between 45 percent and 70 percent of children who are exposed to domestic violence are also victims of abuse, and 40 percent of child victims of abuse are also exposed to domestic violence. Children may be "inadvertently" hurt through domestic violence. They may be hit by items thrown by the batterer, and older children may be hurt trying to protect their mothers.

Children who grow up witnessing domestic violence are seriously affected. Frequent exposure to violence in the home predisposes children to social and physical problems, and it teaches them that violence is a normal way of life. This increases the risk of becoming society's next generation of victims and abusers.

In 1989, Kendall Segel-Evans wrote *Wife Abuse and Child Custody and Visitation by the Abuser*. Children are used by batterers to manipulate their victims. A batterer may threaten to take custody of or kidnap the children if the victim reports the abuse. He may also threaten to harm or kill the children. He may tell the victim that she will lose custody if she seeks a divorce because she "allowed" the abuse to happen. He may even harm the children to control the mother. During and after separation, batterers continue to use these tactics. Visitation and joint custody provide the batterers with opportunities to abuse, threaten, and intimidate their former partners.

Children who are exposed to physical or mental abuse suffer adverse reactions on their physical and mental states, which may affect their educational experiences. Many children are victims of child maltreatment, peer and sibling victimization, and parental abuse. Victimization by family offenders is highest for the youngest victims (Davis, Lurigio, and Herman 2013). These children often suffer in their educational pursuits. Children have been kept in cages or killed by their abusive parents.

Violence against women occurs in various forms and crosses economic and cultural boundaries regardless of class, religion, language, or ethnicity. Battered women come from a wide array of experiences and cultural environments, and they are abused because of age, race, economic status, or sexual orientation. These women are in heterosexual relationships, common-law marriages, or same-sex relationships. Violence against women has existed for centuries.

During the reign of Romulus of Rome, in 753 BC, under the laws of chastisement, it was acceptable for a man to beat his wife. At the end of the Punic Wars in 202 BC, women were given more freedom and could sue their husbands for unjust beatings. In AD 300, the church established husbands' patriarchal authority via the Roman emperor, Constantine the Great, and Jewish law. In the Middle Ages the church continued to sanction abuse of women. Men had permission to beat their wives. If she committed an offense, the man could scold, bully, and terrify her—and beat her soundly with a stick (Hart &Walker, Stevenson and Love 1999).

In the 1500s, according to British common law, a man could beat his wife with a rod not thicker than his thumb. In 1871, Alabama became the first state to rescind the legal right for men to beat their wives. In 1882, Maryland was the first state to make wife-beating a crime. (Freud and Johnson 1998).

Attitudes toward the beating of women took a major turn in 1993. It took 112 years for Congress to pass the Violence against Women Act. Even with this law, violence against women and children still exists. The national incident-based reporting system collected data from nine states and found 53 percent of domestic violence cases involved spouses, 49 percent involved ex-spouses, and 42 percent involved boyfriends, common-law spouses, or partners in same-sex relationships (Brent-Goodly 2001). Intimate partner violence against African Americans is 2.5 times greater than the rate of violence against women of other races.

When masculinity is associated with aggression and sexual

conquest, domineering sexual behavior and violence become not only a means of structuring power relationships between men and women, but also a way of establishing power relations among men.

Many women, men, and children suffer in silence due to embarrassment, low self-esteem, fear, and feelings that they deserve it. Distorted vision makes them forget they are swans with strong wings.

Embarrassment keeps many women from exposing abuse and violence. They do not want family or friends to know about the violence. Some victims have no self-worth and believe they deserve the abuse. They totally depend upon the abusers and believe the perpetrators will not love them without the punishments. Many victims fear for their safety or their lives if the violence is exposed or if they leave the abuser. Threats often isolate victims from their friends and families. If they decide to stay, they may focus on spiritual strategies, resilience, financial security, and hopes that the situation will improve (Davis 2002).

Some women do not leave because they do not want to lose custody of a child or children. Others have nowhere to go. Shelters for abused women are not always available. Many women are concerned about the opinions of others and believe their reputations will be tarnished because they exaggerated or provoked the violence (McGee 2004).

Prostitutes are often beaten or verbally harassed. Physical escape is often not possible. Domestic violence is often brought into housecleaning, babysitting, entertainment, sports, and business. Domestic violence can happen to anyone—regardless of race, age, sexual orientation, religion, or gender. Domestic violence affects people of all socioeconomic backgrounds and education levels. Domestic violence occurs in opposite-sex and same-sex relationships and can happen to intimate partners who are married, living together, or dating. Domestic violence affects those who are abused, and it has a substantial effect on family members, friends, coworkers, witnesses, and communities. Historically, the law has been reluctant to define women as victims when the crimes committed against them take place in the home or as part of a relationship. For centuries, men benefited from not being held accountable for their crimes against women. Since the 1970s, violence against women has been considered a crime.

NCADV (2012) suggests men who abuse women may exhibit some of the following characteristics and behaviors:

- view women as property
- exhibit low self-esteem
- blame behavior on external causes, bad days, alcohol, or drugs
- deny the severity of the problem
- feel jealous, possessive, demanding, or aggressive
- are unemployed
- were abused as children
- have strong, traditional patriarchal beliefs
- tend to overact
- often use force or violence to solve problems
- cycle from being hostile, aggressive, and cruel to being charming, manipulative, and seductive

Unrealistic expectations of marriages and relationships can create distorted vision and lead to reaching for the golden ring in everyday life experiences.

Are women subordinate to men? Some argue that there is no known society where women are superior. Women are often seen as vulnerable, but they are capable of physical labor. This type of profiling is part of distorted vision. Women have always been strong individuals. They display warrior characteristics. Women are rarely portrayed as having strength and courage. Some women's accomplishments are ignored.

The Dahomey, kingdom, which is now known as the Republic of Benin, was created in 1600. It is a small state in West Africa. King Houegbadja (1645–1685), the third son of King Adalja (1709–1732), established an army of female bodyguards. These women were armed with muskets and spears and called themselves N'Nonmiton. They were also referred to as Ahosi ("king's wives") or Mino ("our mother") and were assigned as the king's protectors. They were referred to as

"Amazon women". Their motto was "Conquer or Die." They were not allowed to marry or have children while they were soldiers (Dash 2011, Macdonald 2018) (Amy McKenna, 2015, New Word Encyclopedia, 2018).

Throughout history, women have shown strength and leadership. The Dahomey Amazon women were strong and fierce warriors. These women were called amazons by the Europeans who highlighted these women as warriors. Many of these women disguised their appearances and fought in wars as men. After being killed in battle, their identities were revealed. These women were classified as heroines, but many were condemned as traitors, murdered, or exiled.

I am not advocating violence against violence, but I do advocate both the predator and the victim must seek help. The distorted vision of the predator and the victim's self-esteem can be changed with professional help, but the transformation will not be fast or easy. The pattern that is endured by many individuals is not deserved and will leave physical and mental scars. To obtain peace, there must be forgiveness by the victim and the predator.

Dag Hammarskjold stated, "Friendship needs no work." "The pursuit of peace and progress cannot end in a few years… The pursuit of peace and progress—with its trials and errors, as well as its successes and setbacks—can never be relaxed or abandoned (Shafik, 2011).

Another form of distorted vision is *femicide*. This term was first used in England in 1801. In 1848, it was included in *Wharton's Law Lexicon*. In 1970, the feminist movement worked to bring awareness to this oppression. Femicide, a sex-based hate crime, is killing females because of their gender. Most of the violence occurs in the home.

The World Health Organization calls for training of health workers, mortuary staff, and medical examiners. Data can help personnel in different areas, improve health care and understanding, and address violence against women (Roux 2017).

Nationally, domestic violence leads to estimate two million injuries and 1,300 deaths per year. A pilot program by the Chicago Police Department, State Attorney Kim Foxx and the Chicago Department of Family and Support Service is targeting households that have a high risk of domestic violence. The program links victims to social and legal services. The program focuses on Logan Square and will expand to the South Side of Chicago (McNamee 2014). The emphasis has been on female victims of domestic violence and abuse, including punching, kicking, biting, and spitting.

Many people stay in relationships for the sake of children. Some abusers yell, scream, threaten, induce fear, insult, demean, isolate, lie, withhold information, and control all the finances. Many people feel dependent on their abusers. Some women abuse men by calling them cowards, impotent, or failures. Others falsely accuse or threaten to accuse their partners of assaulting them or their children.

The Centers for Disease Control and Prevention released data that 5,365,000 men and 4,741,000 women had been victims of intimate partner violence.

Some abusers have common characteristics:

- rushing into a relationship and claiming it is love at first sight
- extreme jealousy
- unrealistic expectations or demands
- isolation (cutting off ties to victim to keep the victim completely centered on the abuser)
- force during sex
- drinking to cope with stress
- poor communication skills
- using charm to influence others

Three personality disorders are linked to emotionally abusive behavior:

- narcissistic personality disorder (the perception of being grandiose and requiring the admiration of others)
- antisocial personality disorder (disregarding the rights of others and the rules of society)
- borderline personality disorder (feeling empty, inappropriate, angry, or paranoid)

A New Lens

I prefer to be true to myself, even at the hazard of incurring the ridicule of others rather than to be false, and to incur my own abhorrence

—Frederick Douglass

Everyone must have a clear vision of themselves before judging the behavior of themselves. Seeking help if a situation becomes violent or abusive is essential. Become aware of your own self-worth, value, and uniqueness.

In 1961, Hannah Arendt explained why the act of judging competing values and norms must always be undertaken in dialogue:

> "The power of judgment rests sometimes on a potential agreement with others and the thinking process judging what is reality and what is fantasy. A larger of minds in understanding one's self. "In whose place" one must think perspective one must take into consideration and without whom it ever can operate in all."

The constant problem of predators taking advantage of women, men, and children is universal. Umoja is a village in the grasslands of Samburu, Kenya, where only women can live. The village was founded in 1889 by a group of fifteen women who had been raped by British soldiers. It has grown to include women who have been victims of domestic violence, rape, child marriage, and female genital mutilation. Rebecca Lolosoli is the founder and matriarch of Umoja. Forty-seven women and two hundred children live in the village. These women have created a clear vision of the golden ring of life (Faith Karimi, 2019).

Having pride in one's heritage and accepting who you are with pride and respect is the first step toward clearing the lens. Applying respect to others is the second step. Understanding that the world does not center on you is the third step. The fourth step is developing an open and respectful mind that supports the strategic action of not ignoring the voices of others who are interested in your success in life.

Becoming aware of and accepting circumstances occurring in one's life help an individual become aware of reality. The process helps one understand how to become awake in an unrealistic, make-believe world. There is no single solution for resolving a distorted vision. There are several steps to take, and the steps are different for everyone. Everyone must look inside themselves with clear vision on a regular basis.

An individual should try to move through life with confidence, faith, love, motivation, and aspiration. Everyone should look at situations with clear and unbiased points of view. These positive moments enable one to build a mental ladder and get closer to the golden ring. Some individuals miss the golden ring and fall off the ladder. Others look down and think there is no use in trying. Other people look up, get up, and try again. Those who get up and grasp the golden ring, understand its value and appreciate it. These individuals grow from their experiences, understand the faults and successes, and acknowledge and accept who they are.

Actions are guided by choices, and choices must be made with a clear lens and not with distorted vision. They must understand where they are in life and keep an eye out for obstacles and illusions when seeking the golden ring.

Conclusion

"A successful man is one who can lay a firm foundation with the brick's others have thrown at him."
—David Brinkley

This book explores a brief glance into the author's life, but it also examined various ways that having distorted vision can affect self as well as others. Patterns of negative behavior can be driven by distorted vision and are not always displayed in the same ways. People must find their own ways into the light and clear their own paths. Some individuals need professional help or spiritual consultations to assist in their pursuit of a clear vision. Before any resolution can be made in seeking the golden ring, people must look inside themselves and remain true to what they see.

No one is physically or mentally perfect. Everyone must come to grips with their own demons and fantasies and accept them before a clear lens can be formed. There are several steps to help a person find a clear vision of the world. First, it is important to be tolerant and respectful. Second, it is important to have self-esteem. Third, it is important to have constant open communication. These three steps may enable an individual to discard their distorted vision. However, there so many more steps one can develop on their own as they progress toward having a clear lens.

Some individuals confide in spiritual leaders or medical professionals. Professional consultations and even medications can help resolve certain problems. I am happy to say that prayer and faith helped me learn to accept my demons and love myself. I have forgiven my aunt for the abusive behavior she forged against me as a child. I loved my aunt even thou she committed abusive behavior towards my grandmother and me. I am happy to say I developed a close relationship with my dad and his new wife before their passing.

Before my father's death, I became acquainted with my brother and sister. I developed a closer relationship with my brother than with my sister. With the help of my granddaughter I am happy to say she located my brother's son. If you allow a distorted vision to keep taking you back into a lifestyle that is tinted with pain and sorrow, the golden ring will swing farther and farther away from your reach. But if you understand what caused the hurt or sorrow and turn the hurt and sorrow into learning tools, you will develop renewed steps of life and the golden ring will come closer and closer to you.

I dearly miss my mother. During the time she came to live with me we became very close. The ability to care for my mother was a blessing. Those days were special to me because my mother was in a home where she was loved.

I feel very renewed to look back upon my life now. Through the pains and disappointments in my life, I learned to move forward with a clear vision and hold on to the golden ring. My steps toward a path of overcoming pain and sorrow were not taken alone. My family and friends were my banisters, and God was the steps of my faith I climbed upon every day. I am happy to say with many helpful hands that came into my life and the grace of God I obtained my Bachelor of Arts, a Master of Library Science, and a Doctor of Philosophy. I believe if you seek a path of faith, hope, joy, and love, you will develop a clear vision of life that will often lead you to unexpected rewards.

Notes

1. Annuals of Congress 434 (1789). Madison proposed language limiting the power of the state in a few respects, including a guarantee of freedom of press, Id at 435. Although passed by the House, the Senate, supra, 957, defeated the amendment. At the convention on Monday, September 17, 1787, Present the States of New Hampshire, Massachusetts, Connecticut, MR Hamilton from New York, New Jersey, Pennsylvania, Delaware, Maryland, Virginia, North Carolina, South Carolina, and Georgia.
2. House of Representatives, Subcommittee on Crime, Terrorism and Homeland Security Committee on the Judiciary. September 30, 2009). Cyberbully and other online safety issues for children. Washington, DC.
3. *Reno v. American Civil Liberties Union*, 521 U.S. 844 (1997).
4. *West Virginia State Board of Education v. Barnette*, 319 U.S. 624 (1943).
5. Quid pro quo (en.m.wikipedia.org).

Appendix A

Bullying: Seeking Power over Others

topbully.gov explains various elements of bullying among school-aged children. Bullying is unwanted, aggressive behavior that involves a real or perceived power imbalance. The behavior is repeated or has the potential to be repeated. Kids who are bullied and those who bully others may have serious, lasting problems.

To be considered bullying, the behavior must be aggressive and include an imbalance of power and repetition. Kids who bully use their power—physical strength, access to embarrassing information, or popularity—to control or harm others. Power imbalances can change over time and in different situations—even if they involve the same people.

Bullying behaviors happen more than once or have the potential to happen more than once. Bullying includes making threats, spreading rumors, physical and verbal attacks, and exclusion.

Appendix B

Types of Bullying

Verbal bullying is saying or writing mean things. Verbal bullying includes the following:

- teasing
- name-calling
- inappropriate sexual comments
- taunting
- threatening to cause harm

Social bullying, sometimes referred to as relational bullying, involves hurting someone's reputation or relationship. Social bullying includes the following:

- leaving someone out on purpose
- telling other children not to be friends with someone
- spreading rumors
- embarrassing someone in public

Physical bullying involves hurting a person's body or possessions. Physical bullying includes the following:

- hitting

- kicking
- pinching
- spitting
- tripping
- pushing
- taking or breaking someone's things
- making mean or rude hand gestures

Where and When Bullying Happens

Bullying can occur during or after school. While most reported bullying happens in the school building, a significant percentage also happens on the playground or the bus. It can also happen traveling to or from school, in the neighborhood, or on the internet.

Frequency of Bullying

There are two federal sources of data on youth bullying:

- The 2011 Youth Risk Behavior Surveillance System (Centers for Disease Control and Prevention) indicates that 20 percent of students in grades nine to twelve have experienced bullying.
- The 2008–2009 School Crime Supplement (National Center for Education Statistics and Bureau of Justice Statistics) indicates that 28 percent of students in grades six to twelve have experienced bullying.

Cyberbullying

Cyberbullying is bullying that takes place using electronic technology. Electronic technology includes cell phones, computers, tablets, social media, text messaging, chat rooms, and websites.

Kids who are cyberbullied are often bullied in person as well. Kids who are cyberbullied have a hard time getting away from the behavior. Cyberbullying can happen twenty-four hours a day, seven days a week, and reach a kid who is alone. Text messages and images can be posted anonymously and distributed quickly to a very wide audience. It can be difficult or impossible to trace the source. Deleting inappropriate or harassing messages, texts, and pictures is extremely difficult.

Effects of Cyberbullying

Cell phones and computers are not to blame for cyberbullying. Social media sites can be used for positive activities—connecting with friends and family, helping with school, and entertainment—but these tools can also hurt people. Whether done in person or through technology, the effects of bullying are similar.

Kids who are cyberbullied are more likely to do the following:

- use alcohol and drugs
- skip school
- experience in-person bullying
- be unwilling to attend school
- receive poor grades
- have low self-esteem
- have health issues

Frequency of Cyberbullying

The 2008–2009 School Crime Supplement (National Center for Education Statistics and Bureau of Justice Statistics) indicates that 6 percent of high school students have experienced cyberbullying.

The 2011 Youth Risk Behavior Surveillance Survey finds that 16 percent of high school students were electronically bullied in the past year.

Research on cyberbullying is growing. However, because kids' technology use changes so rapidly, it is difficult to design surveys that accurately capture trends.

Appendix C

Internet Usage

Table 1. Reported Internet Usage for Individuals Three Years and Older, by Selected Characteristics: 2011

(in Thousands)

Selected characteristics	Total	Individual lives in household with internet use[1]		Individual accesses the internet from some location[2]			
		Number	Percent	Number	Percent	Number	Percent
				Access	From Some	Location	
Individuals 3 years and older	293,414	224,349	76.5	204,596	69.7	187,050	64.1
Age							
3–17 years	62,138	49,544	79.7	37,419	60.2	34,163	55.0
18–34 years	71,210	56,091	78.8	58,378	82.0	52,287	73.4
35–44 years	39,478	32,755	83.0	32,144	81.4	30,008	76.0
45–64 years	80,947	63,289	78.2	58,630	72.4	54,911	67.8
65 years and older	39,641	22,671	57.2	18,026	45.5	16,582	41.8
Race and Hispanic origin							
White alone	233,672	182,653	78.2	166,238	71.1	154,129	66.0

71

White non-Hispanic alone	190,318	155,496	81.7	142,827	75.0	134,121	70.5
Black alone	37,117	23,467	63.2	22,370	60.3	18,967	51.1
Asian alone	13,891	12,134	87.4	10,194	73.4	9,801	70.6
Hispanic (of any race)	47,114	29,689	63.0	25,648	54.4	21,943	46.6
Sex							
Male	143,780	110,996	77.2	99,739	69.4	91,994	64.0
Female	149,635	113,353	75.8	104,857	70.1	95,956	64.1
Household income							
Less than $25,000	70,352	35,327	50.2	35,020	49.8	27,940	39.7
$25,000-$49,999	76,985	54,654	71.0	49,070	63.7	43,848	57.0
$50,000-$99,999	89,514	80,448	89.9	71,509	79.9	68,349	76.4
$100,000-$149,999	33,157	31,641	95.4	28,810	86.9	28,097	84.7
$150,000 and more	23,407	22,279	95.2	20,187	86.2	19,717	84.2
Region							
Northeast	52,720	42,237	80.1	37,698	71.5	35,344	67.0
Midwest	63,575	49,269	77.5	45,620	71.8	42,078	66.2
South	108,353	79,002	72.9	72,694	67.1	65,764	60.7
West	68,766	53,842	78.3	48,585	70.7	44,764	65.1
Total 15 years and older	243,689	185,133	76.0	177,808	73.0	163,391	67.0
Employment status							
Employed	140,696	116,894	83.1	114,744	81.6	106,579	75.8
Unemployed	14,711	10,485	71.3	11,126	75.6	9,503	64.6

Not in labor force	88,282	57,755	65.4	51,937	58.8	47,310	53.6
Total 25 years and older	201,475	151,247	75.1	142,374	70.7	131,773	65.4
Educational attainment							
Less than high school graduate	24,960	11,154	44.7	7,864	31.5	6,568	26.3
High school graduate or GED	61,952	41,343	66.7	36,358	58.7	32,786	52.9
Some college or associate degree	53,255	42,880	80.5	42,980	80.7	39,439	74.1
Bachelor's degree or higher	61,308	55,870	91.1	55,171	90.0	52,980	86.4

Source: US Census Bureau,
Current Population Survey,
July 2011

[1] At least one member of the individual's household reported using the internet from home.

[2] "Some location" means internet access that occurs either inside or outside the respondent's home.

Age of Householder	Presence of a Computer	Presence of the Internet	No Internet
15–24	49.4	44.4	55.6
25–34	62.5	57.2	42.8
35–44	70.0	62.7	37.3
45–54	66.9	60.9	39.1
55–64	56.2	49.8	50.2
65 years and over	28.1	23.6	76.4

Appendix D

Ownership

There are several challenges and concerns relating to ownership of email messages, graphic images, and web pages. Are there laws to ensure you own the material you place on the internet? Even though the message was created in a business, library, or a school, the question often voiced is "Who owns the material?"

As stated in the Copyright Act (17 USA 102a-106), internet authors own their material. Schools own or lease the servers and pay for the leases of the lines that allow students, faculty, and staff to have access to the internet. Exception to the law may include issues of copyright infringement. A person who uploads another's work onto his or her website may have committed copyright infringement.

In 1998, Congress passed the Digital Millennium Copyright Act (DMCA) to strengthen copyright protection in the digital age (Roberts 2004). The DMCA prohibits a person from de-scrambling or scrambling work or decrypt an encrypted work without the authority of the copyright owner. If certain violations occur in libraries, schools, or universities, restrictions may or may not be enforced. A school has the legal right to restrict use of the internet; school administrators may consider the rights to freedom and freedom of speech and decide not to restrict internet use, especially at the university level (Johnson and Groneman 2003).

Violations when using the internet can have dangerous

implications. Although the information individuals send on the internet, according to the copyright act, is considered the authors' work, there are ethical and safety issues that can be challenged.

There is a major challenge for the new generation of internet users to understand how the Homeland Security Act and the Patriot Act can impact their ability to transmit information in cyberspace. It is important that the rules and regulations are clear and can be disseminated to individuals so there will be no violations when submitting email messages or any other communication transmissions. Businesses, libraries, and schools need to understand the rules and regulations of the Homeland Security Act and the Patriot Act so they can inform their patrons, staff, students, and teachers.

Appendix E

Safety

In 1996, Congress passed the Communication Decency Act to protect minors from pornography on the internet. This act made it a crime to transmit any obscene or indecent messages to individuals under the age of eighteen. In 2002, the Supreme Court struck down the Child Pornography Protection Act. Argued on March 19, 1997, *Janet Reno v. American Civil Liberties Union* filed the first suit concerning the internet.

Justice John Paul Stevens said, "It is no exaggeration to conclude that the content on the internet is as diverse as human thought." Justice Stevens continued, "Speech on the internet deserves the First Amendment protection ... The internet is a vast library."

On June 26, 1997, the Supreme Court held that (1) provision of the CDA prohibiting transmission of obscene or indecent communications by means of telecommunication device to persons under age eighteen, or sending patently offensive communications through use of interactive computer service to persons under age eighteen, were content-based blanket restrictions on speech, and, as such, could not be properly analyzed on the First Amendment challenge as a form of time, place, and manner regulation; (2) challenged provision were facially overbroad in violation of the First Amendment (Tedford and Herbect 2001).

On June 26, 1997, the United State Supreme Court issued a

sweeping reaffirmation of core First Amendment principles and held that communications over the internet deserve the highest level of Constitutional protection. "The vast democratic fora of the internet" merit full constitutional protection and will also serve to protect libraries that provide their patrons with access to the internet. The Court recognized the importance of enabling individuals to receive speech from the entire world and to speak to the entire world. The Court upheld the rights of freedom of speech and the rights of children.

In 1998, Congress passed the Child Online Protection Act, which applies to commercial websites that are harmful to minors. This act requires commercial online content providers either have actual knowledge that they are dealing with a child twelve years of age or under or who aim their content at children to obtain verifiable parental consent before they can collect, archive, use, or resell any personal information pertaining to that child (American Library Association 2005). The American Library Association (2005) said, "This act also includes any personal information that can be used to contact the child, including email address, full name, home, address, telephone numbers, etc."

The United States v. American Library Association (2003) upheld a federal law requiring public libraries to install software filters on their computers to screen out sexually explicit material that would harm minors (Savage 2004). The American Library Association (2003) states that the use of filtering software by libraries to block access to constitutionally protected speech violates the Bill of Rights. The problem with blocking or filtering information may have some problems:

> A role of librarians is to advise and assist users in selecting information resources. Parents and only parents have the right and responsibility to restrict their children's access—and only their children access to library resources, including the internet.

According to Tedford and Herbect (2001), in the *Mainstream Loudown v. Board of Trustees of the Loudown Virginia Country Library* (1998), the library board adopted a "policy on internet sexual harassments" requiring that software be installed on library computers to "block child pornography and obscene material [hardcore pornography]."

The court struck down the policy. The policy challenged required filters on all library computers where adults or children used them:

> The court rejected the policy and ruled that filters might be appropriate if installed on computers designated only for children ... the issue of filters, in other words, remains contested First Amendment ground.

This ruling applies to public libraries, although most schools have software to protect students. Bauman (2003) states, "In 2003, the Business Software Alliance and *Weekly Reader* developed "Play It Safe in Cyberspace." The program targets children in grades three through eight. The goal of the curriculum is to help elementary and middle school students develop an understanding of ethics, respect intellectual property, and practice responsible computer behavior.

References

Alfano, S. "Internet Press Freedom Conference." Word Press Freedom Committee, 2003.

Ambrosino, Roberto, Joseph Hefferman, and Guy Shuttesworth. *Social Work and Social Welfare*. 7th ed. Belmont, CA: Brook/Cole: Cengage Learning, 2013.

American Library Association. 2004. *USA Patriot Act and Libraries*. ala.org/aka/washoff/woissues/civil liberties. Accessed February 4, 2005.

American Library Association. "USA Patriot Act and Related Measures That Infringe on the Rights of Library Users." American Library Association,2002.

American Library Association.,. "American Library Association Code of Ethics." *Information Power*. American Library Association, 1993.

Anderson, Craig, A., et al. "The Influence of Media Violence on Youth." *Physiological Science in the Public Interest* 4, 2003.

Douglas, Archer. "Intellectual freedom since 9/11. The USA Patriot Act, ETC." *Indiana Libraries* 21, no. 2, 2002.

Arendt, Hannah. "Between Past and Future: Six Exercises in Political Thought", New York: Viking Press, December1961.

Bauman, Jeffery. "Play It Safe in Cyberspace." *Tech Trends: For Leaders in Education and Training* 46, no. 6., 2002.

Bindel, Julie. "The Village Where Men Are Banned." Guardian. www.theguardian.com. Accessed March 10, 2018.

Burton, R. A.2. *Social Psychology*. Pearson. 2012.

Clayton, Mosher, and Scott Akins. *Drugs and Drug Policy: The Control of Consciousness Alteration*. Sage, 2007.

Dash, Mike. *Dahomey's Woman Warriors*. Smithsonian.com. September 23, 2011.

Davis, Robert, et al.. *Victims of Crime*. Sag3, 2013.

Edward, Richard L. "Domestic Violence." *Encyclopedia of Social Work* 19, no. 1, 1995.

Evans, Dabney P. 2015. "Why Do Women Need Special Laws to Protect Them from Violence?" Emory University. theconversation. com. Accessed February 20, 2018.

Freyd, Jennifer, and J. Q. Johnson. *Commentary: Domestic Violence, Folk Etymologies, and "Rule of Thumb."* University of Oregon. 1998, jif@dynamic.uoregon.edu,

Glasser, Ira. "The Struggle for A New Paradigm: Protecting Free Speech and Privacy in the Virtual World of Cyberspace." *Nova Law Review* 627.nd.

Hart, B. "Legal Road to Freedom." *Stress and Emotion, Anxiety, Anger, Curiosity* 15. 1993.

Heise, Lori, et al. "Violence, Sexuality, and Women's Lives." In *the Gender/Sexuality Reader*, 1997.

KeJohnson, Vin, and Nancy Groneman. "Legal and Illegal Use of the Internet; Implications for Educators." *Journal of Education for Business* 7, March 31, 2010.

Kaye, Stephen. 2000. "Computer and Internet Use among People with Disabilities." *Disabilities Statistic Report* 13, March 2000.

Karomi, Faith. "She Grew Up in a Community Where Women Rule and Men Are Banned. *CNN*. January 30, 2019.

Leroux, Carolyn. Understanding and Addressing Violence against Women." Pan-American Health Organization. theconversation.com/why-home-even-when-theres-war-is-the-most-dangerous-place-for-women. Accessed November 28, 2017.

Macionis, John. *Society the Basic*. Pearson., 2017.

Mascoa, Francis E. *Gender and Difference in a Globalizing World: Twenty-First Century Anthropology*. Waveland Press, 2010.

McCullagh, Declan. "US Homeland Security to Policy the Net." *Net Networks*. Sf.indymedia.org/news/. Accessed February 26, 2005.

Macdonald, Fleur. "The Legend of Benin's Fearless Female Warriors", August 27, 2018, www.bbc.com.

McGee, Susan. "Why Battered Women Stay." *Stop Violence*, 2004, Stopviolence.com/domviol/whytheystay.htm.

McKinnon, Catherine A., and Reva. B. Siegel, eds. *A Short History of Sexual Harassment: Direction in Sexual Harassment Law*. Yale Press, 2003.

McNamee, Elizabeth T. "Keep Moving Forward in Fight to Combat Domestic Violence." *Chicago Sun-Times*, 2013.

Mill, John Stuart. *Facial and Political Philosophy: Classic and Contemporary Readings*. Oxford University Press, 2008.

Morales, Frank. "Homeland Security Threatens Civil Liberty: Media Democracy in Action", *Censored 2004*, Seven Stories Press. 2003.

Newsome, Deborah, and Samuel Gladding. *Clinical Mental Health Counseling in Community and Agent Settings*. Pearson. July 22, 2014.

Rakes, Glenda. *Using the Internet*, Minnesota Institute of Public Health, 1996.

Sason, J. *Power of Human Imagination*. Siger and Polk, 1978.

Schriender, K. C., and Lynne Roberts. "DeCSS Code on the Internet: It Is Protected Speech." *The Computer and Internet Lawyer* 24, no. 2, 2004.

Shafik, Assel, *Global Peace Lovers*. Bloomington, Indiana: Authors House, 2011.

Stevenson, Tamain, and Cinci Love, "Herstory of Domestic Violence: A Timeline of the Battered Women's Movement." *Safe New Work*, 1999.

Tracy, Natasha. "Emotional Abuse of Men: Men Victims of Emotional Abuse Too." *Healthy Place*. healthyplace.com. Accessed March 2018.

Tedford, Thomas, and Dale Herbect. *Freedom of Speech in the United States*. Strata Publishing Inc., 2013.

US Census Bureau. 2004. "2001 Presence of a Computer and the Internet in Households." *Statistical Abstract of the United States: 2004–2005.*

US Department of Justice. "What is Stalking?" *Office on Violence against Women.* Justice.gov. Accessed February 2, 2018.

Wallace, John, and Jerald Backman, "Explaining Racial/Ethnic Difference in Adolescent Drug Use: The Impact of Background and Lifestyle." *Social Problems* 38, 1991.

Walker, Lenore, "Three Stages of the Cycle of Violence." In *the Battered Women.* Harper and Row, 1979.

About the Author

D r. Gayles Evans is a retired assistant college professor. She holds a BA, MLS, and PhD. She received her degree in library science from Chicago State University and her doctorate in curriculum and instruction from the University of Illinois at Chicago. A former children's and public and academic reference librarian, Gayles also studied art at the Art Institute at Chicago and was a performance voice major at the American Conservatory of Music.

Dr. Gayles Evans is the author of *The Trunk*, a young adult novel.